Julius Caesar CORIN REDGRAVE

Corin Redgrave began his professional career as an actor/
director in 1961 at the Royal Court Theatre in London, in Tony
Richardson's production of *A Midsummer Night's Dream*. His
most recent parts include Hirst in Harold Pinter's *No Man's
Land* at the National Theatre, Old Jolyon in *The Forsyte Saga*
(Granada TV), and Edward Heath in Jimmy McGovern's
Sunday (Channel 4).

He is a founder member of Moving Theatre, and an associ-
ate artistic director at Houston's Alley Theatre.

As author he has written four plays for BBC radio; a
memoir, *Michael Redgrave: My Father* (RCB/ Fourth Estate);
and is a contributor to *British Cinema in the 1950s* (Manchester
University Press, eds Ian MacKillop and Neil Sinyard).

Colin Nicholson is the originator and editor for the Actors on
Shakespeare series published by Faber and Faber.

CORIN REDGRAVE

Julius Caesar

Series Editor: Colin Nicholson

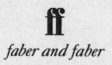

faber and faber

First published in 2002
by Faber and Faber Limited
3 Queen Square London WC1N 3AU

Typeset by Faber and Faber in Minion
Printed in England by Mackays of Chatham plc

A CIP record for this book is available from the British Library

ISBN 0–571–21240–9

10 9 8 7 6 5 4 3 2 1

Introduction

Shakespeare: Playwright, Actor and Actors' Playwright

It is important to remember that William Shakespeare was an actor, and his understanding of the demands and rewards of acting helped him as a playwright to create roles of such richness and depth that actors in succeeding generations – even those with no reason or desire to call themselves 'classical' actors – have sought opportunities to perform them.

As the company dramatist, Shakespeare was writing under the pressure of producing scripts for almost immediate performance by his fellow players – the Lord Chamberlain's Men (later the King's Men), who, as a share-holding group, had a vested interest in their playhouse. Shakespeare was writing for a familiar set of actors: creating roles for particular players to interpret; and, being involved in a commercial enterprise, he was sensitive to the direct contact between player and audience and its power to bring in paying customers. His answer to the challenge produced a theatrical transformation: Shakespeare peopled the stage with highly credible personalities, men and women who were capable of change, and recognizable as participants in the human condition which their audience also shared. He connected two new and important elements: the idea of genuine individuality – the solitary, reflecting, self-communing soul, which is acutely aware of its own sufferings and desires; and, correlatively, the idea of inner life as something that not only exists but can also be explored. For him, the connection became the motor of dramatic action on the stage, as it is the motor of personal action in real life.

The primary importance of the actor cannot be disputed: it is his or her obligation – assisted to a greater or lesser extent by a director's overall vision of the play – to understand the personality they are representing onstage, and the nature of the frictions taking place when that personality interacts with other characters in the drama. Shakespeare's achievement goes far beyond the creation of memorable characters (Macbeth, Falstaff) to embrace the exposition of great relationships (Macbeth–Lady Macbeth; Falstaff–Prince Hal). Great roles require great actors, and there is no group of people in a better position to interpret those roles to *us* than the principal actors of *our* generation – inhabitants of a bloodline whose vigour resonates from the sixteenth century to the present day – who have immersed themselves in the details of Shakespeare's creations and have been party to their development through rehearsal and performance.

Watching Shakespeare can be an intimidating experience, especially for those who are not well versed in the text, or in the conventions of the Elizabethan stage. Many excellent books have been written for the academic market but our aim in this series is somewhat different. *Actors on Shakespeare* asks contemporary performers to choose a play of particular interest to them, push back any formal boundaries that may obstruct channels of free communication and give the modern audience a fresh, personal view. Naturally the focus for each performer is different – and these diverse volumes are anything but uniform in their approach to the task – but their common intention is, primarily, to look again at plays that some audiences may know well and others not at all, as well as providing an insight into the making of a performance.

Each volume works in its own right, without assuming an in-depth knowledge of the play, and uses substantial quotation to contextualize the principal points. The fresh approach of the many and varied writers will, we hope, enhance your enjoyment of Shakespeare's work.

Colin Nicholson

February 2002

Characters

Julius Caesar
Calphurnia, *his wife*
Mark Antony, *his lieutenant*
Octavius, *his nephew*
Lepidus, *triumvir with Antony and Octavius*
Marcus Brutus, Caius Cassius, Casca, Cinna, Decius Brutus,
   Ligarius, Metellus Cimber, Trebonius, *conspirators*
Portia, *Brutus's wife*
Cicero, Popilius Lena, Publius, *senators*
Flavius, Marullus, *tribunes*
Cinna, *a poet*
Young Cato, Lucilius, Messala, Titinius, Volumnius, *friends
   and supporters of Brutus and Cassius*
Claudius, Clitus, Dardanius, Lucius, Strato, Varro,
   Brutus's servants
Pindarus, *Cassius' servant*
Attendants, Citizens, Guards, Senators, Soldiers, Soothsayer

Julius Caesar was performed by the Royal Shakespeare Company at Stratford-upon-Avon in May 1972, with the following cast:

Caius Cassius	Patrick Stewart
Calphurnia	Judy Cornwell
Casca	Gerald James
Cicero	Patrick Godfrey
Cinna	John Atkinson
Dardanius	Tim Pigott-Smith
Decius Brutus	Philip Manikum
First Citizen	John Bardon
Julius Caesar	Mark Dignam
Lepidus	Raymond Westwell
Marcus Antonius	Richard Johnson
Marcus Brutus	John Wood
Marullus	Clement McCallin
Metellus Cimber	Tim Pigott-Smith
Octavius Caesar	Corin Redgrave
Portia	Margaret Tyzack

Directed by Trevor Nunn

Foreword

I have had three working encounters with *Julius Caesar*. In the first I played Octavius Caesar at the RSC in 1972; then Brutus at the Young Vic in 1986, and then Julius Caesar at Houston's Alley Theatre in 1996, a production that I also directed. This essay is a balance sheet of those experiences, or perhaps an interim report on a series of encounters that I hope to resume. The questions it poses are mainly theoretical, concerning problems of interpretation, rather than practical. Anyone seeking a practical guide to the play would do well to consult John Ripley's excellent *Julius Caesar on Stage in England and America*. Published in 1980, its survey ends, in fact, in 1972 with the RSC production I mentioned above, so clearly a great deal of the Tiber's water has flowed under the bridge since then. Nevertheless it is thorough, entertaining and very useful. I happily borrowed certain pieces of business from Ripley's account of the Saxe Meiningen and Beerbohm Tree productions. The Victorians were prolific inventors of stage business, refined and altered to taste and handed on from one generation to the next.

My recollection of the 1972 production is somewhat blurred by the passage of time; but one memory remains distinct. For anyone who saw John Wood as Brutus it will appear, in what follows, how much my understanding of that complex character owes to his performance. When I came to play the part, fourteen years later, I could still hear his voice, and at certain moments I know that my reading followed his as clearly as my voice would allow. Even now, thirty years later, I still cannot imagine how I or anyone could improve on that fine, defiant shout of

Fates, we will know your pleasures.
That we shall die, we know; 'tis but the time
And drawing days out, that men stand upon.
(Act III, scene i)

I have never heard such notes before or since, except from the German tenor Fritz Wunderlich.

The other sharply focused memory is of Patrick Stewart as Cassius, and in particular his delivery of Cassius' soliloquy at the end of the second scene, beginning: 'Well, Brutus, thou art noble . . .' As will be seen later in this essay, I believe that Cassius has been much misinterpreted by actors and scholars alike, and whilst interpretation is a subjective question, in this case a good deal of what is misinterpreted rests on a radical failure to construe correctly the meaning of this soliloquy. For these insights I am indebted to Trevor Nunn.

I thought then that Nunn was one of the best directors I had worked with; but that was after only nine years' experience as a professional actor. Today, after forty years, I would say he is closer to my ideal than anyone I know, and it still feels like an affront that someone of his genius should have been moved to resign by a combination of critics – or 'crritics!', as Estragon might have said in *Waiting for Godot* – and journalists who should have known better. Nevertheless I felt that the decision to dress our production in antique Roman togas made the play unnecessarily remote from its audience. It relieved them of the responsibility to choose, to take sides, to engage with the story in such a way as would call their own sympathies and antipathies into play.

No doubt mine was a very '1970s' response. Post-modernism had yet to be invented, which would reduce all such conflicts as that between the conspirators and Caesarism to a gladiatorial contest, in which the best man, presumably, always wins.

I was at this time becoming active politically. It was the year of the Bloody Sunday massacre in Derry, of Bangladesh's struggle for independence, of the first of two miners' strikes, and of the National Industrial Relations Act, under which three London dockers were jailed. I was as active as I could be, holding meetings, and selling my party's newspaper, the *Workers' Press*. I tried, without much prospect of success, to persuade the RSC's company and staff to join a proposed one-day strike called by the TUC to release the dockers. The strike was called off, thanks to the intervention of a person never before heard of called the Official Solicitor, who released Bernie Steer and the others; but I became, in some quarters, quite unpopular, and no attempt was made to keep me on at the RSC when my contract expired the following year.

I didn't act in Shakespeare again until David Thacker asked me to play Brutus at the Young Vic. I have written elsewhere of what I owe to Thacker, who rescued me from oblivion. Like one or two other fine directors who have young families to raise, he now works only in film and television. It is a terrible loss to the theatre, and I wish he were able to return. His production was staged in the round, a convention I love, and, after a short, inconclusive flirtation with modern battledress, in mid-seventeenth-century costume. Our programme's cover showed a masked headsman raising aloft a severed bearded head, which might have been Caesar's, or Charles I's. This was – in respect of the beheading – a little misleading. Brutus refers to cutting Caesar's head off, but only metaphorically.

> Our course will seem too bloody, Caius Cassius,
> To cut the head off and then hack the limbs,
> Like wrath in death and envy afterwards;
> For Antony is but a limb of Caesar.
>
> (Act II, scene i)

And besides, chopping heads off onstage is a tricky business. Amongst Elizabethan and Jacobean dramatists only Cyril Tourneur, that virtuoso poet and dramatist, rises to the challenge. D'Amville, hero of *The Atheist's Tragedy*, aims his sword against an opponent who ducks, so that the sword completes its journey and decapitates D'Amville himself. Not content with this amazing auto-da-fé, Tourneur has D'Amville speak his dying words through the lips of his severed head.

By situating the play visually in a context some half a century later than its first performance, Thacker evoked the only occasion in England when men and women debated, in all earnestness, the morality of assassination as an instrument of politics. Cromwell's words to the yeomen farmers and artisans enlisted under him are astonishing, even now, both for their audacity and their straightforward matter-of-factness: 'I will not cozen you by perplexed expressions in my commission about fighting for King and Parliament. If the King chanced to be in the body of the enemy, I would as soon discharge my pistol upon him as upon any private man; and if your conscience will not let you do the like, I advise you not to enlist yourselves under me.'*

Any historical analogies demand the greatest caution. The regicides acted against Charles I only after they had defeated his army. Execution then was a means of pre-empting any attempt, with foreign assistance, to restore him to the throne. Brutus and Cassius' assassination of Caesar is nearer to an act of desperation. They were confronting a dictatorship that had absolutized all political power into its own hands, and was using it to crush its opponents. Assassination, then, like other forms of terrorism, was a weapon of last resort, all other forms of redress having been blocked off.

* Cited in Guizot, *History of Charles I and the English Revolution*, translated by Scoble (1854).

Perhaps that was how matters looked to some, at least, in 1599; but therein lay the special interest of the story of Julius Caesar. Certain moments in history are like nodal points in which the strands of preceding periods, and those from periods yet to come, are all gathered together. In the figure of Cromwell, Martin Luther joins hands with Robespierre. By the same process of fusion, Brutus and Cassius join hands with Cromwell in Shakespeare's play.

So, as I sat down in Houston, in December 1995, and gathered my notes for rehearsals of *Julius Caesar*, I read again Christopher Hill's writings on Puritanism and the English Revolution, his biography of Cromwell, *God's Englishman*,* and Antonia Fraser's excellent biography, *Cromwell, Our Chief of Men*.†

My sister Vanessa and I had come to Houston because Greg Boyd, the Alley's artistic director, had invited our company to join with his in productions of *Julius Caesar* and *Antony and Cleopatra*. What resulted from that juncture was an international company in which our ideal of cross-casting would begin to take shape. Antony, Cassius, Octavius, Decius Brutus and Metellus Cimber were played by Afro-Caribbean and African-American actors, David Harewood, Howard Sadler, Aryon Bakare, Ewart Walters, and Alex Alan Morris; Cleopatra by Aicha Kossoko from Benin; and the leader of the plebeians by Tony Scordi from Cyprus. To them, and to the Alley and Moving Theatre companies, and to the companies of the RSC and Young Vic productions, I owe the inspiration for the ideas expressed here.

* Christopher Hill, *God's Englishman*, Weidenfeld and Nicolson, 1970.
† Antonia Fraser, *Cromwell, Our Chief of Men*, Phoenix Press, 1973.

The Crowd

As W. H. Auden says, 'first things, in Shakespeare, are always important',* and first things in *Julius Caesar* are the plebeians, the crowd. They are good-natured enough at first sight, in Act I, scene i, but they have no business to be out in the streets, so their mere presence is ominous. There was no right of assembly in Rome in 44 BC, or in London in AD 1599 (nor in London nor Genoa in AD 2001, when anti-capitalist demonstrations provoked furious assaults by the police). Tribunes, in ancient Rome, had the right to summon *contiones* – semi-spontaneous gatherings of the lower orders at which controversial matters could be aired. But this gathering has not been authorized.

Rome, in fact, was never a democracy, although there were some democratic elements in its constitution and its laws. Its leading citizens had once enjoyed a high degree of liberty, and regarded the enjoyment of liberty as the central element of their lives; but Rome's poorer classes made the mistake of never insisting on those political rights which, had they been won, might have created a more democratic society. They never, for instance, demanded any fundamental changes in the oligarchic procedures that governed the *concilium plebis*, one of the two sovereign assemblies. These assemblies 'allowed no debate, were subject to all kinds of manipulation, and employed a system of voting that was heavily weighted in favour of the wealthy'.†

* W. H. Auden, *Lectures on Shakespeare*, Faber and Faber (2000).
† 'Rome the Suzerain', in G. E. M. de Sainte Croix, *The Class Struggle in Ancient Greece*, Duckworth (1981).

However, although the plebeians had no democratic rights to speak of, their leaders, the tribunes, as though to compensate in some measure, had quite exceptional rights and immunities. These included the right to veto any act by a magistrate, to rescue any plebeian menaced by a magistrate, and even the power to arrest and imprison magistrates, up to and including the highest rank, the consuls. Best of all, the tribunes were inviolable; they were immune from arrest, through the supreme right (which they alone enjoyed) of *sacrosanctitas*. This right is about to be violated.

Perhaps because Shakespeare was influenced by his source, but more likely for purposes that seem to spring from the nature of the play, the tribunes in *Julius Caesar* are quite different from the tribunes in *Coriolanus*. Brutus and Sicinius are self-serving bureaucrats; but Flavius and Marullus, the tribunes in *Julius Caesar*, are wholly honourable. What is said of Brutus by Antony at the play's end could equally be said of them. They are motivated by 'a general honest thought / And common good to all', and they are about to suffer most horribly for it.

Most of what we know – or rather think we know – about Rome's lower orders comes to us from Shakespeare, and via Shakespeare from North, Amyot, Plutarch and Cicero, who is unremittingly hostile to the plebeians. Here in *Julius Caesar* the crowd, benign at first encounter, is next seen through Casca's eyes (Act I, scene ii), hooting and clapping their chapped hands, throwing up their 'sweaty night-caps', and uttering 'a deal of stinking breath'. An unflattering portrait, but worse is to follow. By the time that Antony is done with them, in Act III, scene ii, they have become a pack of blood-stained sans-culottes, as cruel and rapacious as any crowd in the worst nightmare of an aristocratic victim of the French Revolution (Act III, scene iii).

At the opening of the play, however, they are peaceable enough, though perhaps a little the worse for drink. Their articulate representatives, a carpenter and a cobbler, are pissed but still jovial. They are respectful – just – to Flavius and Marullus, calling them 'sir', but teasing them unmercifully with a selection of Shakespeare's most execrable puns. They are out on the streets marking a holiday to celebrate Caesar's triumphal return from his wars against Pompey the Great's nephews. This provokes a tirade from Marullus: 'You blocks, you stones, you worse than senseless things! / . . . Knew you not Pompey?'

Caesar's wars, he says, have weakened Rome by spilling the blood of one of her bravest and best families, whereas Pompey's wars enriched Rome with the booty from foreign conquests and the tribute that his captives paid. This would not recommend Pompey to a modern ear; an Elizabethan audience thought differently. Drake's exploits against Spain had made him a national hero (and over seventy years later, the ambassador from the Netherlands told Charles II that of course the Netherlands thought less of him than of Cromwell, and treated him differently, because 'Cromwell was a great man, who made himself feared by land and sea'). In any case, there is another crucial difference: Pompey the Great was a man – i.e. a human being – whereas Caesar has claims to be superhuman.

Rome is still a republic, clinging to republican traditions, and in the republican catechism the cardinal sin was overbearing pride, by which a man might seek to distinguish himself from his peers and stand above them. 'Proud' – *superbus* – is almost always pejorative, most often associated with the hated memory of the Tarquins, the last monarchy in Rome, defeated and driven out by Marcus Brutus's ancestor.

According to custom, a lictor stood in a victorious general's chariot when he rode in triumph through Rome, murmuring in his ear, 'Remember, you are only human,' because the end of a successful war (when a triumphant general entered the city to popular acclaim surrounded by his army) was a time of danger for the established order. This is just such a time; but Caesar, if he has a lictor whispering in his ear, is deaf to his advice. (Caesar's deafness – 'Come on my right hand, for this ear is deaf' (Act I, scene ii) – seems to have been invented by Shakespeare. It is a brilliant invention. It not only contributes to a picture of a dictator who has to be propped up, as Brezhnev or Yeltsin had to be supported at the elbows, but also contributes to his frightening irascibility and sudden mood-swings. He hears what he wants to hear.) Caesar's supporters have decked out the city with busts of Caesar crowned with 'diadems', i.e. imitation crowns. They are inviting the plebeians to accept Caesar as king, and suggesting that he should be worshipped as a god.

FLAVIUS

     let no images
Be hung with Caesar's trophies . . .
These growing feathers pluck'd from Caesar's wing
Will make him fly an ordinary pitch,
Who else would soar above the view of men
And keep us all in servile fearfulness.
  (Act I, scene i)

Julius Caesar is the most public of Shakespeare's plays, and the most political. It examines the uses and abuses of public speech, of rhetoric, and how such speech can influence people and events for better and for worse. It shows two distinct kinds of public speech in action: honourable and dishonourable. In Plato's Athens there were two kinds of philosophers: virtuous philosophers – seekers for truth – and sophists – those mercenaries whose professional skills, on hire to Athens' numerous litigants, could be employed to make 'the worse cause appear the better'. In Shakespeare's Rome two kinds of oratory are similarly distinguished and contrasted. There is honourable public speech, such as used by Flavius and Marullus; and there is dishonourable rhetoric, which is shown to be much the more successful.

As there are two kinds of rhetoric, so there are two parties, or 'interests', each with its own constituency. Caesar's is the crowd, the plebeians. Brutus's and Cassius', the patricians and the equestrians, the men of property. These are not watertight distinctions, and there is overlap in both directions. For instance, respect and admiration for Brutus, Casca says, extend through all classes in society: 'O, he sits high in all the people's hearts . . .' (Act I, scene iii).

Conversely, Caesar by turns seduces, flatters and terrifies the senate, although overall his policy is drastically to reduce their importance and cut them down to size as an independent force in society. Both parties must appeal to the plebeians, who are by far the most numerous class ('the many') and without whose support neither side can hope to gain a lasting victory. Fluid though they are, these distinctions are exceptionally important. Cinna's exultant shout immediately after Caesar's death – 'Liberty! Freedom! Tyranny is dead!'– stirs the blood; but as Engels pointed out in another context, he means liberty for his own class, the men of property. The debates in Cromwell's army on Putney Heath are half a century away. There is no thought as yet that the rights and liberties that are contended for in *Julius Caesar* should be extended to the plebeians. Nor would they be, for another two and a half centuries. Indeed, the most ardent democrat might pause before granting electoral franchise to Shakespeare's mob. As Shelley said, 'The consequences of the immediate extension of the elective franchise to every male adult would be to place power in the hands of men who have been rendered brutal and stupid and ferocious in ages of slavery.'*

In the crucial moments that follow Caesar's assassination, however, no man's voice rings out in sympathy with Caesar's assassins. The senate is paralysed with fear, their panic beautifully epitomized in the pathetic figure of an aged senator, Publius, blindly staggering to and fro, unable to find the exit.

BRUTUS

People and senators, be not affrighted.

Fly not; stand still; ambition's debt is paid.

CASCA

Go to the pulpit, Brutus.

DECIUS

      And Cassius too.

BRUTUS

Where's Publius?

CASSIUS

Here, quite confounded with this mutiny.

METELLUS

Stand fast together, lest some friend of Caesar's

Should chance –

BRUTUS

Talk not of standing. Publius, good cheer;

There is no harm intended to your person,

Nor to no Roman else. So tell them, Publius.

CASSIUS

And leave us, Publius, lest that the people,

Rushing on us, should do your age some mischief.

    (Act III, scene i)

In the space of a few moments the Capitol is deserted, except

* P. B. Shelley, *A Proposal for Putting Reform to the Vote throughout the Kingdom* (1817).

for the small knot of conspirators standing over the body of Caesar, their nerves stretched in anticipation that the mob will rush in and butcher them. Did they expect tumultuous acclaim, like the 'general shout' that greeted Caesar's refusal of the crown in Act I, scene ii, or the 'universal shout' that greeted the triumphant Pompey (Act I, scene i)? Perhaps so; but now, when Caesar's outstretched fingers, reaching for the crown that the senate meant to offer him, have been prevented from grasping it, Rome, instead of hailing Brutus and Cassius as its liberators, is distraught with grief and fear. Trebonius, in a few staccato syllables – 'Men, wives, and children stare, cry out, and run, / As it were doomsday' – describes a city nightmarishly like Moscow in 1953 as imagined by Yevtushenko in the film *Stalin's Funeral* (1990) with its scenes of hundreds of mourners being trampled to death in a blind stampede of grief for the fallen dictator.

Brutus, in his soliloquy, reasoned the need for a preemptive strike against Caesar –

> And, since the quarrel
> Will bear no colour for the thing he is,
> Fashion it thus: that what he is, augmented,
> Would run to these and these extremities;
> And therefore think him as a serpent's egg,
> Which, hatch'd, would, as his kind, grow mischievous,
> And kill him in the shell.

– and a majority of commentators seem to find this repugnant. They want Caesar to have the benefit of the doubt and, like good citizens, insist that he should be presumed 'to be innocent until he is proved guilty'.* The awful irony is,

* Norman Sanders, the editor of the Penguin edition of the play, writes: 'Brutus misapplies logic wilfully, if unconsciously [?] and consequently decides on the basis of supposition and possibility rather than on the proven evidence which points in the opposite direction.'

however, that Caesar's assassination may have come not too early but too late, and if it is in fact too late, the chances of a successful outcome are much less. Indeed, the two central metaphors of the play concern time and tide, and the consequences of missing them.

> Men at some time are masters of their fates . . .
>
> (Act I, scene ii)

and

> There is a tide in the affairs of men
> Which, taken at the flood, leads on to fortune;
> Omitted, all the voyage of their life
> Is bound in shallows and in miseries.
>
> (Act IV, scene iii)

Both Brutus and Cassius understand the need to strike at the appropriate moment; but neither achieves this when it is needed most. This is not to sit in judgement on them, but to state a fact that is central to the play's dialectic. For instance, at the battle of Philippi, Brutus gives his opponents a crucial advantage by striking too soon:

TITINIUS

> O Cassius, Brutus gave the word too early,
> Who, having some advantage on Octavius,
> Took it too eagerly; his soldiers fell to spoil,
> Whilst we by Antony are all enclos'd.
>
> (Act V, scene iii)

Even if Brutus were right to believe that Caesar is only a tyrant *in potentia*, and not a fully developed one, the date chosen, 15 March (the 'ides'), when the senate intends to offer him the crown, would still be the latest moment at which to strike against him. 'For the tyrant in entrance, a significant number agreed, had to be slain as soon as possible, before his tyranny could gain rooting, or worse still, legitimacy through oath and pact.'* All the evidence of this play, however, points to Caesar's crowning as only the completion of a process already far advanced; and the most compelling evidence of all is in the reaction of the people and senators to Caesar's death. Perhaps Cassius was right to rage at the passivity of his fellow Romans:

> Those that with haste will make a mighty fire
> Begin it with weak straws. What trash is Rome,
> What rubbish, and what offal, when it serves
> For the base matter to illuminate
> So vile a thing as Caesar . . .
>   (Act I, scene iii)

* Robert S. Miola, *Julius Caesar and the Tyrranicide Debate*, Renaissance Quarterly 38 No. 2 (Summer 1985), reprinted in *Julius Caesar*, ed. Harold Bloom, Chelsea House Publishers, 1994.

Two Kinds of Rhetoric

Brutus has an impeccably republican pedigree. His ancestor, Julius Brutus, drove the Tarquins from Rome. His uncle and father-in-law, Marcus Porcius Cato, Portia's father, was a man of awesomely unbending principle. Brutus is the 'Soul of Rome', her 'Brave son, deriv'd from honourable loins!' (Act II, scene i). Anchises, father of Aeneas and mythical founder of the Roman race, told his descendants that their destiny was to 'spare the conquered and put down the proud'.* It is a role Brutus seems born to fulfil.

Yet poor Brutus staggers under the weight of his ancestry. It may be his destiny to be Rome's liberator, but he groans under it as an almost intolerable ancestral curse. It forces him to immolate his own personality on the altar of his principles. Portia tells him:

> It will not let you eat, nor talk, nor sleep;
> And could it work so much upon your shape
> As it hath much prevail'd on your condition,
> I should not know you Brutus.
>   (Act II, scene i)

'Honour' and 'honesty' are two words that appear again and again in Brutus's vocabulary. They are like twigs with which to birch himself. They give him no peace, no space to bargain with his destiny. Dante confined Brutus to the lowest circle of Hell for betraying Caesar, his friend; but in the civil war between love and duty that rages within Brutus, duty is bound to prevail. Not because he doesn't feel love – he is a

* 'Parcere subjectos et debellare superbos' (Virgil, *Aeneid*, IV, 847–53).

man of intense feeling. But he has dammed up all sublunary loves in the cause of a higher principle, his duty to his country. The most poignant moment in the play is his promise to himself that he will find the time to mourn Cassius properly – 'I shall find time, Cassius, I shall find time' (Act V, scene iii). He doesn't, of course.

He is unimpeachably honest. His speech to the plebeians in Act III, scene ii is plain and homespun in the extreme. Plutarch in his 'Life of Brutus' calls his style 'Spartan', and it is so, to a fault. Antony pretends to be in awe of Brutus's oratory –

I am no orator, as Brutus is,
But (as you know me all) a plain blunt man,
That love my friend; and that they know full well
That gave me public leave to speak of him.
For I have neither wit, nor words, nor worth,
Action, nor utterance, nor the power of speech
To stir men's blood; I only speak right on.
(Act III, scene ii)

– but, like almost everything Antony says in the market place, this is an ingenious lie. Brutus, as is painfully clear from his first words, has no command of oratory. He scarcely realizes the need for it, or understands that he is entering a contest with a man ten times more gifted as a public speaker than he. Rhetoric – the art of persuasion – Aristotle explains, is composed of logic, the skilful selection of examples, and the ability to be able to judge one's audience and know how to appeal to its emotions. By these criteria, Antony is amply endowed as an orator and Brutus not at all; but then oratory is a Greek art, the Greeks being masters of deceit, and Antony, who wears his hair long, grows his beard, and loves plays and music, is a thoroughly Hellenized Roman. (Christian Meier's fascinating biography,

Caesar, says that Antony 'went to Greece to study rhetoric and train for military science'.*) Brutus is a Roman's Roman. His only weapon is his honesty. It is his armour, and like Pilgrim he trusts to it completely, believing it will shield him from all evil.

> There is no terror, Cassius, in your threats;
> For I am arm'd so strong in honesty
> That they pass by me as the idle wind,
> Which I respect not.
> (Act IV, scene iii)

He builds his speech to the plebeians on the rock of his honesty, using it as the foundation for a simple syllogism: 'Brutus is honest. Honest men speak the truth. Brutus says Caesar was ambitious. It follows that that is a true statement.'

BRUTUS   Romans, countrymen, and lovers, hear me for my cause, and be silent, that you may hear. Believe me for mine honour, and have respect to mine honour, that you may believe. Censure me in your wisdom, and awake your senses, that you may the better judge. If there be any in this assembly, any dear friend of Caesar's, to him I say that Brutus' love to Caesar was no less than his. If then that friend demand why Brutus rose against Caesar, this is my answer: Not that I loved Caesar less, but that I loved Rome more. Had you rather Caesar were living, and die all slaves, than that Caesar were dead, to live all free men? As Caesar loved me, I weep for him; as he was fortunate, I rejoice at it; as he was valiant, I honour him; but, as he was ambitious, I slew him. There is tears, for his love; joy, for his fortune; honour, for his valour; and death, for his ambition . . .
  (Act III, scene ii)

*Christian Meier, *Caesar*, trans. David McLintock, HarperCollins, 1995.

If honesty consists of speaking the truth as one sees it, with no thought of personal gain and regardless of any cost to oneself, this is admirably honest. This honourable rhetoric is even effective, for the moment. The plebeians believe Brutus and applaud him.

FIRST PLEBEIAN
This Caesar was a tyrant.
THIRD PLEBEIAN
    Nay, that's certain.
We are blest that Rome is rid of him.

In the prelapsarian Rome of Brutus's ancestors, that other Eden for which he yearns and to which his plain speaking and his honesty belong, this would have sufficed; but in a Rome corrupted by Caesar's tyranny it is woefully inadequate. Simple logic and unvarnished honesty are no proof against skilful demagogy. Against Antony's skills, honesty is like Ned Kelly's armour: it leaves the wearer vulnerable in the most critical places. Brutus's argument is linked together in a simple chain of reasoning, and like a chain it is no stronger than its weakest link. Antony has only to take one link in the chain – Brutus's assertion that Caesar was ambitious – and test it by offering proofs and examples to the contrary, and the argument falls apart. Its premise, Brutus's honesty, then begins to crumble, because it has been causally linked to statements that no longer seem convincing. They have been tested by counter-examples and found wanting.

It doesn't matter that the proofs or counter-examples that Antony offers are far from perfect and would not survive close inspection. For instance, Caesar's refusal of the crown that Antony offered him at the feast of Lupercal may have been a cynical ploy, a piece of theatre, but it looked like the real thing to the plebeians then, and it passes muster now, in the market place, as an example of Caesar's humility. Likewise Caesar's tears, his sympathy for the plight of the poor – 'When that the poor have cried, Caesar hath wept; / Ambition should be made of sterner stuff' (Act III, scene ii) – may have been genuine or feigned, but it doesn't matter. All that matters is that Antony is arguing and offering reasons. The First Plebeian observes: 'Methinks there is much reason in his sayings'; whereas Brutus, who promised to provide 'reasons' – 'I will myself into the pulpit first, / And show the reason of our Caesar's death' (Act III, scene i) – offers only statements, or assertions, with no proofs to support them. But then, reasoning and argument are not his forte. He deals summarily with any proposals he doesn't like: 'Good reasons must of force give place to better' (Act IV, scene iii); and his authority amongst his followers is so immense that none dares challenge him except Cassius, and he reluctantly. That is both his strength and his downfall.

Both Brutus and Antony love Caesar. In this respect at least, Antony is honest. Both are Caesar's surrogate sons. (Suetonius suggests in his *Lives of the Twelve Caesars* that Brutus was Caesar's natural son, and this legend was well known to Renaissance writers; but Shakespeare doesn't allude to it.) However, it is the prodigal son, Antony, who has the greater purchase on Caesar's affection; and it is Antony who wears his heart on his sleeve in the market place: 'Poor soul! His eyes are red as fire with weeping,' exclaims the Second Plebeian.

Antony wasn't present at the battle where Caesar defeated the Nervii:

> You all do know this mantle. I remember
> The first time ever Caesar put it on;
> 'Twas on a summer's evening in his tent,
> That day he overcame the Nervii . . .
>
> (Act III, scene ii)

21

but it sounds fully convincing. This 'I remember', with its simple but tellingly descriptive details – ''Twas on a summer's evening' – is a stock-in-trade opening for folk singers and story tellers all over the world. No one questions it. It belongs, as of right, to the teller of tales, to ask his audience to believe that 'I was there', and it carries him through to his next imposture, which is to describe Caesar's assassination as if he had been present. We, the audience, know that he wasn't –

CASSIUS
Trebonius knows his time; for look you, Brutus,
He draws Mark Antony out of the way.
    (Act III, scene i)

– but the plebeians don't know this. The description sounds for all the world as though Antony had been a helpless horrified spectator:

Look, in this place ran Cassius' dagger through:
See what a rent the envious Casca made:
Through this the well-beloved Brutus stabb'd . . .
    (Act III, scene ii)

It is a con-trick of course. A slow motion camera might have shown who stabbed Caesar and where, but in the frenzy of his killing no observer could have discerned such details, and would only know that Casca stabbed first and Brutus last. It is superbly convincing, however; and whereas it was Brutus's hope that they would appear as 'sacrificers, but not butchers', Antony succeeds entirely in making them seem butchers, which is how he thinks of them: 'O, pardon me, thou bleeding piece of earth, / That I am meek and gentle with these butchers' (Act III, scene i).

His methods are diabolical; but, as General Booth noted, the devil has all the best tunes. (The actor-manager Sir Herbert Beerbohm Tree (1853–1917) elected, against tradition, to play Antony, and wrote in his notebook: 'For the scholar Brutus, for the actor Cassius, for the public Antony.' He cut the other characters' text savagely, and rearranged the order of the text to ensure that Antony's was indeed the lion's role. Deplorable, but one sees his point.)

Then there is the will. Caesar's bequest – seventy-five drachmas to each Roman, and his gift to the city of his gardens and orchards – is mentioned in Plutarch; but Shakespeare transforms a simple statement of fact into a complex dramatic irony, via the changing meanings of the word 'will', from an intention:

CAESAR

    And you are come in very happy time
    To bear my greetings to the senators,
    And tell them that I *will* not come today.
      (Act II, scene ii)

to a volition:

CAESAR

    The cause is in my *will*: I *will* not come;

to a simple auxiliary to the future tense:

CAESAR

    How foolish do your fears seem now, Calphurnia!
    I am ashamed I did yield to them.
    Give me my robe, for I *will* go.

But in the market place in Act III, scene ii, at the most crucial moment in his oration, with the crowd already three-quarters won over, Antony produces his masterstroke:

ANTONY

    But here's a parchment with the seal of Caesar;
    I found it in his closet; 'tis his will.

With this he completes his conquest of the plebeians, working them into a frenzy:

ANTONY

I fear I wrong the honourable men
Whose daggers have stabb'd Caesar; I do fear it.

FOURTH PLEBEIAN

They were traitors. Honourable men!

ALL

The will – The testament!

SECOND PLEBEIAN

They were villains, murderers! The will! Read the will!

Antony's rhetoric, and the pantomime business with the will, have transformed the crowd into a murderous lynch mob.

Finally, Caesar's testament becomes, in Antony's hands, as mutable an instrument as Caesar's will has been:

ANTONY

But, Lepidus, go you to Caesar's house;
Fetch the will hither, and we shall determine
How to cut off some charge in legacies.

(Act IV, scene i)

A Serpent's Egg*

In imperial Rome, after Caesar's death, Brutus and Cassius were non-persons. Anyone suspected of venerating their memory or their cause would be a marked man. A century later, however, the empire felt itself sufficiently secure to elevate them to the status of harmless icons. Tacitus remarks that busts of the tyrannicides had become fashionable ornaments, like the image of Che Guevara that sold a million T-shirts.†

In the Renaissance, Caesar and his assassination became a subject of fierce debate. Some scholars and divines saw, in the principate of Caesar and the empire of Augustus, the ushering in of the Christian era, and bestowed a quasi-prophetic status upon Virgil, whose fourth *Eclogue* was thought to announce the arrival of the Christian messiah.

The main strand of this debate, however, concerned tyranny, and how to respond to it. Arguments ranged from asserting the duty of passive obedience at one extreme, to the right and duty to armed rebellion and regicide at the other. Classical authors were scoured for all kinds of proofs and tests by which to distinguish a lawful monarch from a tyrant. Aristotle, for instance, describes a righteous monarch as one who regulates relations between the classes in society for the good of all, whereas a tyrant is one who claims to work on behalf of the *demos*, the lower orders, but uses their support

* 'And therefore think him as a serpent's egg / Which, hatch'd, would, as his kind, grow mischievous; / And kill him in the shell.' From Brutus' soliloquy in Act II, scene i.
† Though Guevara's photographer never received a cent for the reproduction of his iconic image until just before his death.

to attack other men's property. (If we substitute the concept of 'good government' for 'righteous monarchy', Aristotle's distinction serves well, even now.)

Later writers introduced further distinctions and classifications. A king, for instance, might ascend his throne lawfully, and rule well for a time, but then degenerate into a tyrant. Conversely, a tyrant might usurp the throne unlawfully but grow into benevolence. (Shakespeare's history cycle provides a wonderful case of this dialectic in the figures of Richard II and Bolingbroke. The latter deposes Richard unlawfully and usurps his throne, but then does penance and rules righteously.) The figure of Caesar was central to this debate, as were those of his assassins. For some, Caesar personifies both kinds of tyranny, i.e. he is a usurper who seizes absolute power unlawfully (*tyrannus ex defecto tituli*); he is also one who uses his power, whatever the lawfulness or not of his claim, to oppress and crush his subjects (*tyrannus ex parte exercitii*).

Caesar's assassination was a popular subject in the Elizabethan theatre. (In *Hamlet*, Polonius refers to an amateur performance, in his youth.) But besides the excitement of the story, the assassination provided a template from which to discuss matters that by the end of Elizabeth's reign were becoming urgent. In 1599, the year of *Julius Caesar*'s first performance, Oliver Cromwell was born. All the conditions that would produce the civil war of 1640, ending in the defeat and execution of Charles I, were maturing at the turn of the century. Elizabeth's rule was under attack from the Puritan left and the Catholic right. Her campaign against the former had produced a punitive act of parliament – the Act against Seditious Sectaries – and several martyrs, including Henry Burrow, John Greenwood and John Perry. Her persecution of Catholics had called down on her the wrath of two Popes. Pius V deposed and excommunicated her, '*pretensa angliae regina*'. Sixtus V accused her of 'exercysinge an absolute Tyrannie'. Recusant literature resounds with these denunciations.

Questions about the legitimacy of absolute monarchy contribute immensely to the form and content of *Julius Caesar*. Though there was no democracy as we would recognize it in Tudor England, nor any memory of such a state, certain statutory rights commemorated the result of earlier struggles. More importantly still, there were a conviction that religious and political liberties were under threat, and the beginnings of a form of radical nostalgia, conjuring up a vision of times past when religious and political liberty were thought to have flourished. Within a generation or less, the phrase 'The Norman Yoke' was coined, expressing the notion that Anglo-Saxon liberties had been trampled on by the Norman Conquest.* Cassius sounds this note early in the play:

> I have heard,
> Where many of the best respect in Rome
> Except immortal Caesar, speaking of Brutus,
> And groaning underneath this age's yoke,
> Have wish'd that noble Brutus had his eyes.
> (Act I, scene ii)

Julian Rome is still – though only just – a republic. Caesar has not yet assumed the crown. Yet everything we see and hear until the moment of Caesar's death suggests that coronation would only complete his tyranny.

First appearances, to borrow from Auden again, are important in Shakespeare's plays because they plunge us straight into the heart of the matter. Caesar's first appearance speaks volumes about the style of his rule, and the enfeebling culture

---

* *Macbeth*, which has the tyranny of James I in its sights, is set in pre-Norman times and contrasts Macbeth's tyranny with the benign rule of Edward the Confessor.

of deference it has instilled in those around him. His progress towards the games has all the pomp and ceremony of a royal procession. All around comport themselves like janissaries at the court of a Turkish despot, thumping their chests with their forearms, like helmeted supporting players in a Hollywood epic circa 1951. There are Casca's 'Peace ho! Caesar speaks.', and Antony's 'When Caesar says, "Do this," it is perform'd,' and Cassius' 'Fellow, come from the throng; look upon Caesar.'

As Caesar returns from the games, Brutus notices his courtiers' cringing fear of his displeasure:

> But look you, Cassius,
> The angry spot doth glow on Caesar's brow,
> And all the rest look like a chidden train.
>
> (Act I, scene ii)

Soon after we hear that the tribunes have been 'put to silence':*

CASCA Marullus and Flavius, for pulling scarfs off Caesar's
images, are put to silence.
(Act I, scene ii)

The offhand way in which this news is conveyed, between a joke about Cicero speaking Greek and a reference to Caesar and Antony's 'foolery', is chilling. Casca is a nervous, twitchy humorist and 'put to silence' is a macabre joke. The tribunes represent – 'speak for' – the people, and have dared to speak in public against Caesar. No other character is so outspoken. Even Cassius, Caesar's most passionate opponent, is circumspect:

* Some commentators question whether this means that the tribunes have been killed. I do not believe it is in doubt. Cf. Webster's 'I am in the way to study a long silence.'

CASCA

'Tis Caesar that you mean, is it not, Cassius?

CASSIUS

Let it be who it is.

(Act I, scene iii)

Brutus says that Caesar was killed for 'supporting robbers', i.e. for corruption and nepotism; but the criticism comes after Caesar's death, in Act IV, scene iii. Until that moment Brutus could not admit, even to himself, any such fault in Caesar. It is a brilliant insight into the degree of self-censorship men impose upon themselves under a dictatorship. But the tribunes accused Caesar, in a public place, of murdering Pompey's nephews. Silencing them puts an end to any vestiges of free speech.

The appalling charade in the senate, in Act III, scene i, shows the result. Caesar begins the proceedings regally. He and 'his' senate will hear petitions:

CAESAR

Are we all ready? What is now amiss
That Caesar and his senate must redress?

Metellus Cimber presents his petition, asking for clemency for his vanished brother. Caesar was famous, in particular, for two qualities, both of which would be familiar to an educated Elizabethan audience: his *celeritas* (speed of thought and decision) and his *clementia* (clemency). Shakespeare turns these completely upside down. The statesman who famously made up his mind in a trice is shown to be a vacillating neurotic. The 'merciful' Caesar is portrayed as immovably bent upon his revenge. No reasons are given for Publius Cimber's banishment, nor are any offered for refusing to grant a pardon – only a paranoid rant about Caesar's will being unchangeable, which is all the more disturbed and disturbing because we sense it lacks any commensurate objective source, but springs from Caesar's anxiety, his need to preserve his own self-created image. The image, however, needs constant refurbishment because it suits so poorly with his actual behaviour. This man, who longs to believe in his own adamantine will, is actually riddled with anxiety and childishly suggestible.

At the first production of *Richard II*, Elizabeth is said to have exclaimed that Shakespeare's portrait of its deposed and murdered Richard resembled herself. Richard, like Caesar, banishes without cause – or for a trumped-up cause – and like Caesar, brooks no appeal for clemency:

RICHARD

It boots thee not to be compassionate;
After our sentence plaining comes too late.

(Act I, scene iii)

Richard is allowed to regret his mistake. Not so Caesar.

Cassius and Brutus: an Appraisal

'History is written by the victors.' Mark Antony has imposed his view of the defeated on our thinking:

> This was the noblest Roman of them all.
> All the conspirators save only he
> Did that they did in envy of great Caesar;
> He only, in a general honest thought
> And common good to all, made one of them.
>   (Act V, scene v)

Yet this justly famous speech, with its generous praise for a fallen opponent, is no less calculating than Antony's funeral oration for Caesar. In 'Friends, Romans, countrymen . . .', Antony makes no distinction between Brutus and his followers:

> Here, under leave of Brutus and the rest,
> (For Brutus is an honourable man,
> So are they all, all honourable men)
>   (Act III, scene ii)

and that 'all', repeated for emphasis at the caesura, ensures that each of the conspirators shares collective responsibility for Caesar's murder.

In his epitaph, however, Antony distinguishes Brutus from the other conspirators. Though he is not relieved of responsibility for Caesar's murder, he is absolved of any blame in respect of his motives:'This was the noblest Roman of them all. / All the conspirators save only he . . .' This 'all', repeated from the end of the first line at the beginning of the next, dissociates Brutus from the collective guilt. (There is however, an ironic shift of emphasis. The first 'all' offers unqualified praise, as if to say that Brutus was unrivalled amongst all the Romans; the second narrows the scope to include only 'all the conspirators'.)

Like a card sharper who fans a deck of cards, saying 'Pick any card you like,' whilst actually forcing the card of his choice upon us, Antony prompts us to accept his version of an altruistic Brutus, and 'forces' us to accept uncritically his condemnation of Cassius and the rest as selfish opportunists. He thus achieves an improbable triumph. Without mentioning Caesar or his execution – he says only, in a tactful circumlocution, that the conspirators 'did what they did' – he rehabilitates Caesar. The paranoid sclerotic tyrant has been restored to his plinth, like one of the ruins that Cromwell knocked about a bit, only a little the worse for wear.

How many millions of essays have been set in school, 'comparing and contrasting' Brutus with Cassius, basing the comparison on Antony's epitaph? 'Brutus is . . . idealistic, impractical . . . a poor judge of character, a hopeless tactician . . . but *honourable*. Cassius is . . . envious, a schemer, ipso facto *dishonourable*.' Thus Caesar's murder becomes, instead of the most daring, apocalyptic event in Renaissance drama, merely one in a wearisomely familiar roll-call of hubristic adventures, like Lady Bracknell's French Revolution – 'and you know what that unfortunate event led to'.

We collude in this because our vocabulary is deficient. We cannot even name Brutus, Cassius, Casca, Cinna, Decius Brutus and Metellus Cimber without using Antony's term 'the conspirators', a term that, as Brutus recognizes, carries a surcharge:

> O conspiracy,
> Sham'st thou to show thy dangerous brow by night,

When evils are most free? O, then by day
Where wilt thou find a cavern dark enough
To mask thy monstrous visage?
 (Act II, scene i)

But Brutus, once he has made up his mind, overcomes his distaste for secrecy:

what other bond
Than secret Romans, that have spoke the word,
And will not palter?

We – democrats of the twentieth and twenty-first centuries – are less tolerant. We have lost the nineteenth century's terms of reference and its generosity. *Pace* Lady Bracknell, Victorian England had a warm heart for those who fought tyranny. They associated Brutus and Cassius with the Decembrists, the Narodniks, or the Garibaldini. Swinburne said that Brutus was 'the very noblest figure of a typical and ideal republican in all the literature of the world'. The twentieth-century view was less generous. Orson Welles, whose modern-dress production at the Mercury Theatre in New York set *Julius Caesar* in the context of a fascist dictatorship, describes Brutus in a programme note as 'the classical picture of the eternal, impotent, ineffectual, fumbling liberal; the reformer who wants to do something about things but doesn't know how and gets it in the neck in the end. He's dead right all the time, and dead at the final curtain.'*

If Mark Antony's epitaph has reinforced a certain view of the conspirators – 'All the conspirators save only he / Did that they did in envy of great Caesar' – Caesar's speech to

* Quoted in John Ripley, *Julius Caesar on Stage in England and America*, Cambridge University Press (1980).

Antony in Act I, scene ii beginning 'Yond Cassius has a lean and hungry look . . .' has imposed itself upon all but a few critics as the definitive view of Cassius. Norman Sanders, editor of the Penguin edition, writes that 'this description is as accurate as can reasonably be expected . . . personally, his hatred of Caesar is grounded in envy at beholding a greater than himself . . .'

Sanders seems to have overlooked the fact – which is surely not negligible – that when he says this, Caesar has just ordered his most influential opponents, the tribunes, to be put to death, very painfully ('put to silence' implies that they have been garrotted, or had their tongues burned out). We should be hesitant, I think, about accepting Caesar's view of Cassius. We should also question the charges Caesar makes against Cassius:

> He reads much,
> He is a great observer, and he looks
> Quite through the deeds of men. He loves no plays,
> As thou dost, Antony; he hears no music.

It is natural enough, perhaps, that Caesar fears Cassius, as an intellectual who analyses men's actions. That Cassius 'loves no plays' and 'hears no music' allies him with the 'seditious sectaries' whom Elizabeth had outlawed. Puritan dislike for choral singing and polyphony was well known. The Puritans wanted to complete what had been begun by the Reformation, which silenced compositions such as those of the Scottish composer Robert Carver, whose complex vocal tapestries were sung in church in the first half of the sixteenth century. The man who has 'no music in himself' is 'fit for treasons, stratagems and spoils'.*

* *The Merchant of Venice*, Act V, scene i.

I am not sure whether Cassius 'loves no plays'. We have Caesar's word for it, but one doubts whether it should be given any more weight than the rest of Caesar's charges. Soon after Caesar's assassination, Cassius seems as proud as Brutus to think that it will be portrayed by generations of actors in the future.

> How many ages hence
> Shall this our lofty scene be acted over,
> In states unborn, and accents yet unknown!
> (Act III, scene i)

This doesn't sound like a man who hates the theatre. Some Puritans, such as William Prynne, author of *Histrio-Mastix*, loathed the theatre, as much for social or class reasons – because it was the playground of the wealthy – as because its representations were lewd or immoral. But Prynne had suffered abominably for his beliefs, having had both his ears cut off and his nose slit, and deserves some indulgence for his iconoclasm. In any case, Cassius doesn't resemble him, even remotely.

Cassius *is* a puritan, however. Caesar's description, however partial, is accurate in this respect. As a puritan, every aspect of his sensibility is affected by beliefs that are simultaneously religious, political and philosophical. He is clearly on the far side of that 'dissociation of sensibility' which Eliot suggested separates those who came after the metaphysical poets from their predecessors.* His speech is short, stabbing and monosyllabic. He rarely trusts himself in metaphor.

Cassius is a follower of Epicurus, the Greek philosopher whose luminously rational beliefs were explored in *De rerum natura* by the Latin poet Lucretius. In place of superstition,

---

* T. S. Eliot, 'Metaphysical Poets', *TLS* (20 October, 1921).

they looked for natural causes in all phenomena. This puts Cassius in the vanguard of that shift of consciousness in England at the beginning of the seventeenth century, which would put an end to some of the most painful relics of medievalism. Cassius is all too readily assimilated into a strain of villainy whose most daring representative is Edmund in *King Lear*. Like Edmund, he confides in the audience in soliloquy, and makes them a partner in his deception. Ergo, he is assumed to share Edmund's villainy. The Penguin editor writes: 'Cassius has a philosophy more Renaissance than Roman, and which, to Shakespeare's original audience, was personified by the imperfectly known but notorious figure of Niccolo Machiavelli.'

Machiavelli was among the first to articulate the proposition that the end justifies the means; but *Julius Caesar* inhabits a moral dimension very different from that of the Italian philosopher, who undertook to instruct princes in the art of keeping their heads. In *Julius Caesar*, ends and means exist in a complex, difficult relationship where both are subject to a higher judgement. For instance, Cassius' letters:

> I will this night,
> In several hands, in at his windows throw,
> As if they came from several citizens,
> Writings, all tending to the great opinion
> That Rome holds of his name; wherein obscurely
> Caesar's ambition shall be glanced at.
> And after this, let Caesar seat him sure,
> For we will shake him, or worse days endure.
> (Act I, scene ii)

This is a deception certainly, but a rather curious, childish deception. He is successful – Brutus is taken in and believes they have been written by different people – but one reason

Brutus believes this is that Roman citizens *have* been leaving anonymous letters for him to find, calls to action against Caesar: 'Such instigations have been often dropp'd / Where I have took them up.' And although they deceive Brutus, Cassius' letters are not instrumental in persuading him to join the conspiracy and lead it. Brutus has already made up his mind to do so, before Lucius appears with the letters. At the very beginning of this scene, in the first line of his soliloquy in the orchard, Brutus has already convinced himself of the need to kill Caesar.

> It must be by his death: and for my part,
> I know no personal cause to spurn at him,
> But for the general. He would be crown'd:
>> (Act II, scene i)

It is a remarkable use of soliloquy. Rather than working towards a conclusion, Brutus states his conclusion unambiguously in the first line. This means that the thought has been present in his mind for some time, as Brutus himself implies in his first conversation with Cassius in Act I, scene ii:

> What you would work me to, I have some aim:
> How I have thought of this, and of these times,
> I shall recount hereafter.

Is it possible that this incident with the letters, including Cassius' naïve belief that they will do the task of convincing Brutus, and his exultant cry at the end of the soliloquy – 'And after this, let Caesar seat him sure, / For we will shake him, or worse days endure.' – is a palimpsest, a survival from an earlier draft? It would not be the only case. Messala's apostrophe to Error in Act V, scene iii belongs in manner, if not in content, to an earlier play; and the two accounts of Portia's death in Act IV, scene iii, which some editors believe to be correct, seem to me like a pentimento, an earlier draft surviving alongside a later version.

However, the difficulty of Cassius' forged letters is nothing compared to the difficulty that the first part of Cassius' soliloquy has caused editors and actors alike. Robert S. Miola, author of the excellent essay, 'Julius Caesar and the Tyrannicide Debate', writes: 'In a soliloquy early in the play Cassius makes a sinister observation: "Well, Brutus, thou art noble; yet I see / Thy honourable mettle may be wrought / From that it is dispos'd." He rejoices at the success of his plot in language that suggests corruption and deceit.' To paraphrase Cicero, men may construe speeches after their fashion, clean from the purpose of the speeches themselves. Cassius' whole soliloquy is predicated upon the hypothesis that, though Brutus, as an honourable man, understands and is inclined – 'disposed' – to fight against Caesar, nevertheless, as Caesar's friend, he may be persuaded – 'seduced' – away from the path of duty:

> Well, Brutus, thou art noble; yet I see
> Thy honourable mettle may be wrought
> From that it is dispos'd; wherefore 'tis meet
> That noble minds keep ever with their likes;
> For who so firm that cannot be seduc'd?
> Caesar doth bear me hard; but he loves Brutus.
> If I were Brutus now, and he were Cassius,
> He should not humour me.
>
> (Act I, scene ii)

To construe this speech after Miola's fashion must imply that Cassius believes he is 'seducing' Brutus to commit a wicked or dishonourable action, an assumption that is clearly gainsaid by everything that has preceded this soliloquy, and everything that follows it. Brutus only invites Cassius to speak about Caesar on condition that Cassius has an honourable end in view:

BRUTUS

But wherefore do you hold me here so long?
What is it that you would impart to me?
If it be aught toward the general good,
Set honour in one eye, and death i' th' other,
And I will look on both indifferently;
For let the gods so speed me as I love
The name of honour more than I fear death.

CASSIUS

I know that virtue to be in you, Brutus,
As well as I do know your outward favour.
Well, honour is the subject of my story.

It would be a rash man indeed, after an overture like that, who would proceed to incite Brutus to the killing of Caesar, unless he were convinced that Brutus would think it honourable. And Brutus does think it entirely, absolutely honourable. What else is the scene with Caius Ligarius intended to convey?

LIGARIUS

I am not sick if Brutus have in hand
Any exploit worthy the name of honour.

BRUTUS

Such an exploit have I in hand, Ligarius,
Had you a healthful ear to hear of it.

(Act II, scene i)

Cassius and Brutus are brothers-in-law (Cassius is married to Brutus's sister, Junia). They went to the same school, where their schoolfellows included Casca and Volumnius. This upbringing is interesting. They are bound together, not only by ties of affection, but by shared principles and a common outlook. Brutus is a Stoic, Cassius an Epicurean. All are convinced republicans. Schools and universities played an

39

immense role, as did preachers, in preparing men's minds for the Puritan revolution. Thomas Beard, for instance, Cromwell's schoolmaster in Huntingdon, who wrote plays that Cromwell was said to have acted in, published a famous book, *The Theatre of God's Judgement*, in 1597, two years before the first performance of *Julius Caesar*. It depicts a struggle between good and evil in which those who are saved fight for God. Beard laments 'how rare good princes have been at all times'. God's punishment awaits 'the mighty, puissant and fearful'.* Beard says that 'the greatest and mightiest princes are not exempt from God's punishment in their iniquities'.

Cassius' Epicurean statement of faith – that 'Men at some time are masters of their fates' – is likewise a Puritan conviction, belonging in spirit completely to Beard's teachings in *The Theatre of God's Judgement*. Puritanism roused men from their passivity, by challenging the doctrine of passive obedience. It rescued men from the enfeebling snare of fatalism, taught them to be up and doing, awoke the spirit of inquiry, and lauded the supremacy of reason over superstition. Above all, it said that if they were to gain victory, they must not fear defeat.

* 'Fearful' here means one who strikes fear into others, not one who is afraid.

Aftermath

Neither Brutus nor Cassius has any notion of what will follow the execution of Caesar, nor what sort of government or constitution will replace Caesar's. They have no theory to guide them, nor even any expectations – only the general wish that things should return to where they were before Caesar rose to power. They march towards the future with their eyes fixed on the past, on a Rome that was long ago liberated by the heroic deeds of their forefathers.

In this respect they are more typical, as revolutionaries, than is perhaps generally thought. Every revolution until the twentieth century was dragged backwards into the future. The revolutions of the eighteenth and nineteenth centuries went into battle against the established order not so much to create a new world as to restore the old one and reclaim those rights which had been taken away; but the revolutions of 1793 and 1848 had some light to guide them, a theory derived in part from previous revolutionary experiments. The English revolution of the seventeenth century had to grope its way forward by candlelight. 'I can tell you, sirs,' Cromwell told two members of parliament in 1641, 'what I would not have, though I cannot what I would.'

Looked at from the twenty-first century, it seems improvident of Brutus and his comrades to have embarked on such a hazardous course of action with so little thought of what was to follow. Generations that have been reared on *Animal Farm* and the proposition that revolutions only replace one form of dictatorship with another will approve the sentiments of the Third Plebeian:

SECOND PLEBEIAN

If thou consider rightly of the matter,
Caesar has had great wrong.

THIRD PLEBEIAN

Has he, masters?
I fear there will a worse come in his place.
(Act III, scene ii)

In this instance he is right, of course. Caesar's assassination, like Kirov's assassination in 1934, is followed by a reign of terror under the triumvirate of Antony, Octavius and Lepidus more terrifying than anything of Caesar's. Messala reports

That by proscription and bills of outlawry
Octavius, Antony, and Lepidus
Have put to death an hundred senators.
(Act IV, scene iii)

A Fabian, such as Shaw, would have held Brutus and Cassius responsible for that; but it is doubtful whether Shakespeare's audience would. 'Duties are ours, events are the Lords,' said the Puritan Samuel Rutherford, using the term 'event' in its proper sense of 'outcome', 'that which comes after'. This formidably simple logic comes in a direct line from the Huguenots. It is Brutus's thinking also, before the start of the battle of Philippi:

O, that a man might know
The end of this day's business ere it come!
But it sufficeth that the day will end,
And then the end is known.
(Act V, scene i)

It is this perspective – that 'events are the Lords' – that makes Brutus, of all the conspirators, especially scrupulous about tactics and the relationship of means to ends. *Some* means are unavoidable; for instance, secrecy. It is distasteful to have to contrive in secret, but Caesar's dictatorship leaves them no choice. But where there is a choice to be made between expediency and principle, he chooses principle. Thus he rejects Cassius' proposal that they should kill Antony:

> Our course will seem too bloody, Caius Cassius,
> To cut the head off and then hack the limbs,
> Like wrath in death and envy afterwards;
> For Antony is but a limb of Caesar.
> Let's be sacrificers, but not butchers, Caius.
> We all stand up against the spirit of Caesar,
> And in the spirit of men there is no blood.
> O, that we then could come by Caesar's spirit,
> And not dismember Caesar! But, alas,
> Caesar must bleed for it. And, gentle friends,
> Let's kill him boldly, but not wrathfully;
> Let's carve him as a dish fit for the gods,
> Not hew him as a carcass fit for hounds.
>
> (Act II, scene i)

No speech of Brutus's has attracted more censure than this. For some, like Orson Welles (see above), for whom revolutionary expediency was the highest and indeed the only criterion – 'whatever is for the revolution is good, whatever is against it is bad' – Brutus's refusal to sanction force against Antony, and his naïve belief that they can win Antony to their side – 'I know that we shall have him well to friend' – deserves scorn. Others accuse Brutus of pious self-deception – 'Let's kill him boldly, but not wrathfully; / Let's carve him as a dish for the gods' – for portraying a cruel act of murder as a religious ritual. And all commentaries point out that this is the first and worst of a string of tactical errors on Brutus's part, the second being to overrule Cassius and allow Antony to speak at Caesar's funeral, and the third, again overruling Cassius, to fight at Philippi instead of drawing Antony's forces on in a war of attrition.* Fifty years after *Julius Caesar*, Parliament's forces were confronted with the same dilemma: whether to use force or persuasion. The army's left wing, the levellers, wanted to use persuasion, and we judge them sympathetically for it. So, 300 years on, did Alexandra Kollontai's and the workers' opposition. Arguments for and against coercion are likely to have occurred at every moment in history where a minority, acting as a vanguard, and believing that it acted on behalf of the majority, has nevertheless not yet won the majority to it side. Brutus, more than others, is very aware of the need for justice to be seen to be done, which means convincing the majority:

> And let our hearts, as subtle masters do,
> Stir up their servants to an act of rage,
> And after seem to chide 'em. This shall make
> Our purpose necessary, and not envious;
> Which so appearing to the common eyes,
> We shall be call'd purgers, not murderers.

Looking back on the civil war after the restoration of Charles II, with that concentration of mind which Johnson

---

* On this last matter, an Elizabethen audience – at least the educated part of it – would have been critical of Brutus. Rome's military history and the tactics of the Roman army's best commanders were well known. Some would certainly remember that Quintus Fabius Maximus, whose nickname was 'Cunctator' ('the man who plays for time'), saved Rome in the war against Hannibal by refusing to give battle, retreating down the length of Italy, scorching the earth, and finally trapping Hannibal's exhausted army near Bari. Ennius, a poet of whose work almost nothing survives, celebrated the achievement with an epigram: '*unus homo nobis cunctando restituit rem*' ('one man, by playing for time, saved our bacon').

says comes to those who are about to suffer the death penalty, the seventeenth-century regicides regretted that they had not used more, rather than less, force. 'We would have enfranchised the people,' said one, bitterly, 'if the nation had not been more delighted in servitude than in freedom.' Cromwell's saints never thought of themselves as democrats, and never tried to represent their actions in that light. 'The great difficulty', said another, 'is to show how the depraved, corrupted, and self-interested will of man, in the great body which we call the people, being once left to its own free motion, shall be prevailed with to espouse their true public interest.' Even Milton felt compelled, with much difficulty and regret, to justify the use of force.

Brutus's refusal to use force against his opponents and his underestimation of their ruthlessness, for which he is unfairly taxed with priggishness, springs from conviction and principle. So too does his decision to allow Antony free speech. Both mistakes are costly; but they speak to a belief in the benevolence of human nature, and they have New Testament teaching behind them as well as classical authority. 'No one sins knowingly,' was a Socratic principle, meaning that none of us would choose to persist in wrongdoing if we fully understood that what we were doing was indeed wrong.

We are about as distant from Brutus today as it is possible to be. We take pride in being unsentimental to those whom we call 'losers'. Anxieties and insecurities about Britain's long decline from its former pre-eminence have made us cynical about the Olympian ideal. Brutus, an Olympian through and through, suffers from this. Starting with foreknowledge of the failure of his revolution, we are adept at charting the course by which his mistakes lead inexorably towards defeat.

In the context of its time, however, and for some time after, defeat was no shame. What would have been shameful was not to give battle. The blunt force with which Brutus concludes his first discussion with Cassius, with its uncharacteristic colloquialism 'chew upon this', tells how far Brutus will go, and how much he will risk, to avoid such a shame.

> What you have said
> I will consider; what you have to say
> I will with patience hear, and find a time
> Both meet to hear and answer such high things.
> Till then, my noble friend, chew upon this:
> Brutus had rather be a villager
> Than to repute himself a son of Rome
> Under these hard conditions as this time
> Is like to lay upon us.
>
> (Act I, scene ii)

Calvinism was as much a nexus of attitudes, a preparation of the mind and body for struggles to come, as a religion. Such a state of mind gave courage and confidence, justifying a man's actions in this world and making him fit for the next. It is not difficult to imagine how necessary such an outlook might be in a world of terrifying economic and political uncertainty. Knowing that God is on your side must be a powerful asset at any time. For those who needed the courage and resolve to overthrow earthly authority rather than submit to it, it was indispensable.

But how do you know that God is on your side? The answer is that you don't, without undergoing a formidable induction process, a frightening and very lonely series of battles with your conscience – 'wrestling with God', Cromwell called it – and this is exactly where Brutus is at the beginning of the play. This scowling person who admits, Hamlet-like, to having lost all his mirth, rebuffs Cassius because he is locked away in some solitary and private hermitage:

CASSIUS

Will you go see the order of the course?

BRUTUS

Not I.

CASSIUS

     I pray you, do.

BRUTUS

I am not gamesome: I do lack some part
Of that quick spirit that is in Antony.
Let me not hinder, Cassius, your desires;
I'll leave you.

Brutus is 'with himself at war', unable to live with any ease or comfort under Caesar's dictatorship, but uncertain that providence has chosen him to fight against it. This uncertainty continues and deepens until the moment of decision in Act II, scene i. The soliloquy at the beginning of this scene performs the function of a camera zooming in to a close-up. But, unlike the camera, it does not halt at the exterior features, but passes directly to the interior of Brutus's soul. It reveals his condition as one of extreme melancholy, whose causes are political and spiritual. Burton's 'anatomy of melancholy' documents the behaviour of one who suffers from melancholy in its various forms. Portia's description of Brutus's behaviour is like one of Burton's case histories.* Nowadays we would call this manic depression, and think of Brutus as being in the trough of a manic-depressive cycle; but then, most of us lack much experience of the extremes in which Brutus finds himself. Politically his dilemma is acute: to

* Robert Burton, *The Anatomy of Melancholy* (1621).

betray his country or betray his friend, Caesar. E. M. Forster prayed for the courage to betray his country; but, charming though that is and must have been for Forster's friend, one has the feeling that Forster's dilemma is a sort of parlour game. Because when, in the real world, would Forster have been called on to make that choice? But that is Brutus's agonizing choice.

Spiritually his condition is even more complex. If we try to analyse the play in the context of its time, we should locate Brutus's melancholy in that moment of acute depression which, in the Calvinist scheme of things, precedes the access of 'grace', the conversion that occurs when a man knows he is 'elect'. How long such a depression might last could vary from weeks to years. A famous physician, Sir Thomas Mayerne, recalls a consultation with Oliver Cromwell in London in 1628, when he found the latter 'extremely melancholy'. Cromwell's own doctor in Huntingdon, John Symcotts, confirmed that diagnosis a little later, and added that Oliver was hypochondriac. There is an unconfirmed account from about this time that Cromwell was intending to emigrate to New England, where the Pilgrim Fathers had exiled themselves in 1608. Cromwell himself dated his emergence from the 'Slough of Despond' into the bright light of God's grace as occurring in the autumn of 1638. In a letter to a friend written in October of that year he exclaimed: 'Oh, I lived in and loved darkness, and hated the light. I was a chief, the chief of sinners. Oh, the riches of his mercy!'

The sense of being exalted – of a sort of holy glee, of being sure and certain of the path one has chosen – seems to be the reward for the unrelieved depression that precedes conversion. So it is with Brutus. All the minus signs in his temperament are transformed on a sudden, as if a switch has been thrown, into pluses. Where he was reserved and moody before, he's all quicksilver now. His speech 'No, not an oath . . .', in Act II, scene i, rushes forward in an excited torrent. He bathes his comrades in the bright light of his certainty. His insistence that they must trust one another, and not 'stain' their cause or themselves by swearing an oath, is of a piece with Puritan practice. Puritans demanded the right to affirm in a court of law, avoiding oaths whenever possible; and it is because Brutus communicates so strongly his sense of having joined the company of saints that Cassius, Casca, Cinna, Metellus and Decius Brutus allow themselves to be ruled by him without demur.

Both Brutus and Cassius, however, suffer a further crisis of faith at the battle of Philippi. We shall understand this better by looking at the very supple and suggestive way in which *Julius Caesar* treats the question of the supernatural. Caesar, the man of destiny, is enmeshed in the coils of superstition, as were, *mutatis mutandis*, the majority of men and women in Tudor England. Their external world was dominated by forces over which they had little or no control. Superstition helped to mediate nature's blind forces, at the price of confirming their invincible superiority.

Psychologically their fears were tempered by the rituals of Catholicism; but these supports were kicked away by the Reformation. Protestantism placed a great responsibility of choice upon the individual, and prepared a way for science to extend the boundaries of man's control over nature. The figure of Cicero stands midway between the superstition of Caesar and the rationalism of Cassius. Both Cassius and Brutus are firmly on the side of rationalism.

But on the eve of the battle at Philippi, Brutus is visited by the ghost of Caesar. Like Hamlet he demands to know if the ghost is angel or devil. The ghost of Caesar anwers: 'Thy evil spirit, Brutus,' meaning that he has been sent by the

49

devil. Brutus prepares to wrestle with the devil, throwing down a breathtakingly courageous challenge:

BRUTUS
> Why com'st thou?

GHOST
To tell thee thou shalt see me at Philippi.

BRUTUS
Well; then I shall see thee again?

GHOST
Ay, at Philippi.

BRUTUS
Why, I will see thee at Philippi then.
(Act IV, scene iii)

To wrestle with the devil successfully would be a work of grace; but Brutus is denied that. The ghost, returning at Philippi, persuades Brutus to take his own life.

We are so familiar with the convention that Romans disembowelled themselves in defeat by falling on their swords that we easily overlook the fact that neither Brutus nor Cassius holds to this, and Brutus very explicitly repudiates it:

> I know not how,
> But I do find it cowardly and vile,
> For fear of what might fall, so to prevent
> The time of life, arming myself with patience
> To stay the providence of some high powers
> That govern us below.
> (Act V, scene i)

Nevertheless, Brutus is persuaded by Caesar's ghost to kill himself, when the ghost has had its revenge upon Cassius.

O Julius Caesar, thou art mighty yet!

Thy spirit walks abroad, and turns our swords
In our own proper entrails.
(Act V, scene iii)

Cassius' suicide, the finality of their defeat, and a second visit
from his 'evil spirit' make Brutus kill himself.

VOLUMNIUS
What says my lord?
BRUTUS
Why this, Volumnius:
The ghost of Caesar hath appear'd to me
Two several times by night: at Sardis once,
And this last night, here in Philippi fields.
I know my hour is come.
VOLUMNIUS
Not so, my lord
BRUTUS
Nay, I am sure it is, Volumnius.
(Act V, scene v)

Cassius' descent into despair and suicide is predicated on
his crisis of faith. As he confides to Messala:

You know that I held Epicurus strong,
And his opinion; now I change my mind,
And partly credit things that do presage.
(Act V, scene i)

He slides back into superstition, and thence into that state of
melancholy and 'error', in which he kills himself:

MESSALA
Mistrust of good success hath done this deed.
O hateful Error, Melancholy's child,
Why dost thou show to the apt thoughts of men

The things that are not? O Error, soon conceiv'd,
Thou never com'st unto a happy birth,
But kill'st the mother that engender'd thee!
(Act V, scene iii)

The metaphor spins out of control. The verse becomes turgid and laborious, painfully like Bottom the Weaver's dying lament in the play about Pyramus and Thisbe in *A Midsummer Night's Dream*.* One cannot escape the feeling that the ending of *Julius Caesar* is hurried and botched. Are Brutus and Cassius defeated by an accumulation of mistakes, some grave tactical misjudgements, and some elementary errors, like Pindarus's misreading of the situation he sees from the top of the hill? Or are they overwhelmed by a superior force? Cassius' observation 'My sight was ever thick' could have been a potent irony, given that he 'looks / Quite through the deeds of men', according to Caesar, and given the exchange with Brutus that begins: 'Tell me, good Brutus, can you see your face?' But here it is inert, rather than potent. It seems merely to echo the source, Plutarch's 'Life of Brutus' ('Cassius himself saw nothing, for his sight was very bad') – unnecessarily, since it is Pindarus who misunderstands what he sees, not Cassius. And how do Messala and Titinius, finding Cassius' body, know that he killed himself because he blamed himself, wrongly, for Titinius being taken captive? Pindarus has fled, and only he knows why Cassius killed himself. And so on – the questions pile up.

Perhaps the confusions of the ending derive more from the contradictions of this story, as Shakespeare tells it. The spirit of hope, of optimism, that is at the core of the play has

* Perhaps Shakespeare wrote the exchange between Titinius and Messala in Act V, scene iii for the two worst actors in his company – incurable hams – as a punishment.

revealed itself through a story that concludes with a total defeat. It is not difficult to think of parallels, narratives of struggle against tyranny, whose endings are equally grim. The slave revolt of Spartacus, for instance, achieved little or nothing, even for the treatment of slaves, but was an inspiration for later generations. Somewhere between the Renaissance and the nineteenth century we acquired the idea of progress and with it the spirit of optimism. *Julius Caesar* is near to the crossroads of this discovery.

A *Julius Caesar* for Our Time?

> Men at some time are masters of their fates:
> The fault, dear Brutus, is not in our stars,
> But in ourselves, that we are underlings.
>> (Act I, scene ii)

Cassius' daring outburst, that men make their own destinies, has been worn smooth by frequent quotation, which has had the effect of reducing it to an elegant, well-turned statement of the obvious – just what the 18th century thought good poetry should be, but the antithesis of what Shakespeare does. One of the advantages of Shakespeare in the theatre, however, is that we can hear these lines spoken as if new-minted; and when they are, they have a heart-stopping audacity.

Here is a man nerving himself to undertake one of the most hazardous and momentous actions is history, the execution of a tyrant ruler. To carry off such an enterprise required more than physical courage. Men's minds needed to be prepared. A revolution in thought had to precede a revolution in practice, and for this there were certain prerequisites. Kingly authority had to be divested of its semi-divine status. This was what the tribunes Marullus and Flavius were attempting. It is also Cassius' task:

> I cannot tell what you and other men
> Think of this life; but for my single self,
> I had as lief not be as live to be
> In awe of such a thing as I myself.
> I was born free as Caesar; so were you;
> We both have fed as well, and we can both

Endure the winter's cold as well as he:
For once, upon a raw and gusty day,
The troubled Tiber chafing with her shores,
Caesar said to me, 'Dar'st thou, Cassius, now
Leap in with me into this angry flood,
And swim to yonder point?' Upon the word,
Accoutred as I was, I plunged in
And bade him follow; so indeed he did.
The torrent roar'd, and we did buffet it
With lusty sinews, throwing it aside
And stemming it with hearts of controversy.
But ere we could arrive the point propos'd,
Caesar cried, 'Help me, Cassius, or I sink.'
I, as Aeneas, our great ancestor,
Did from the flames of Troy upon his shoulder
The old Anchises bear, so from the waves of Tiber
Did I the tired Caesar. And this man
Is now become a god, and Cassius is
A wretched creature, and must bend his body
If Caesar carelessly but nod on him.
He had a fever when he was in Spain,
And when the fit was on him, I did mark
How he did shake; 'tis true, this god did shake;
His coward lips did from their colour fly,
And that same eye whose bend doth awe the world
Did lose his lustre;

    (Act I, scene ii)

It is astounding how little attention has been given to what was new, indeed revolutionary, in this speech. There is hardly anything to compare with it for simplicity and directness. No fewer than four lines are composed of monosyllables. There are only four words of three syllables and one of four in a speech of forty-one lines. The whole speech is written so as to be spoken at breakneck speed, in a white heat of passion, without the audience losing a syllable of its meaning. This is especially remarkable when it is kept in mind that Shakespeare deploys a vocabulary of 37,000 words, constantly borrowing and fashioning words to give them new meanings, or coining new words and expressions altogether. It is as if, with Cassius, Shakespeare is fashioning a new form of address, whose meaning will be equally accessible to the educated and uneducated. Nothing like this will be heard until the Puritan preachers of the seventeenth century.

It is a puritanism of language and of spirit. Even the reference to Virgil's *Aeneid*, in which the founder of Rome carries his father Anchises from Troy, is self-explanatory, needing no prior knowledge to be understood. There is only one metaphor – 'stemming it with hearts of controversy' – which is so simple it could easily be taken for a statement of fact. There are only very simple similes. Even the image 'His coward lips did from their colour fly', where subject and indirect object are transposed as if in angry haste, achieves a greater clarity than if the normal syntax had been used.

If the language is revolutionary, the thought is even more so. Caesar is a man in all respects like any other, except that he is weaker and more fearful than some. By pointing out how much more mortal Caesar is than he pretends to be, Cassius drives his subjects to measure themselves against him, as they must if they are to rid themselves of being, in John Cook's words, 'enamoured of their servitude'.

Monarchy in Britain became constitutional in 1688. In the last quarter of the twentieth century it debased itself so low that most of us wish it would either recover a little of its lost majesty or depart the scene altogether; but for more than half the world's population, who are still ruled by elected, appointed or hereditary dictatorships, and for whom criticism of the ruler is still a punishable offence, the common humanity of the ruler is very much in question. Even in an officially atheist country such as China, or Cuba, the gerontocracy must occasionally attempt symbolic rejuvenation, like Rider Haggard's She, to preserve their authenticity. Mao Tse Tung, like Caesar, went for a very public swim in the Yangtse in late middle age. Adoring poems were written about Mao's swim; and Fidel Castro who, like Caesar, has lately been afflicted with embarrassing swooning fits, counters suggestions of fainting by having himself photographed running up stairs two at a time.

Yet Cassius' speech has been treated over and again as though it exemplifies Mark Antony's and Caesar's claims that Cassius is motivated by envy. For instance:

> In the Cassius who speaks of greatness in terms of feeding, and of honour in terms of personal achievement, we have the man whose political grasp is limited to immediate practice, whose mind cannot grasp abstract concepts, who can only perceive those standards which he himself creates, and for whom politics is in the realm of personal relationships in which he is naturally inept yet in which he craves success.*

In fact, Cassius' speech is even more audacious and subversive when we consider what Shakespeare is doing to the figure of Caesar. For antiquity and for the Renaissance, Caesar's reputation as a soldier, statesman, writer and lover was matchless. Shakespeare's Caesar is the opposite in every respect of the Renaissance Caesar. In this psychotic bully no trace remains of the historical Caesar's celebrated clemency. Caesar was famed for his *celeritas Caesaris* – that speed of thought with which he

* Norman Sanders, editor of *Julius Caesar*, Penguin (1967).

read a situation and made his decision. Shakespeare's Caesar is hopelessly uncertain. Decius Brutus's portrait of him as a man easily influenced by flattery is clearly to the point. Of Caesar the stylist – that exemplary style which for centuries schoolchildren were taught to emulate – nothing remains except the trick of referring to himself in the third person, which is either pretentiously regal or ridiculous.

This treatment of Caesar outraged Shaw so much that he accused Shakespeare of 'travestying a great man as a silly braggart, whilst the pitiful gang of mischief makers who destroyed him are lauded as statesmen and patriots'. To even the score Shaw wrote *Caesar and Cleopatra*, a very dull play with an even duller hero.

At least Shaw understood Shakespeare's intention correctly, even if he didn't approve of it. Norman Rabkin, in his very influential essay, praises Shakespeare for presenting 'one of the defining moments in world history in such a way that his audience cannot determine whether the protagonist is the best or the worst of men'. Harold Bloom writes: 'There is an extraordinary blend of uncannyness (what is that word supposed to mean?) and vainglory in Shakespeare's Caesar, but the uncannyness and sublimity (ah!) seems to me the stronger element.'

There is ambivalence, certainly, in the complex declension of Antony, from the playboy of the opening scenes, to the brilliant demagogue of the market place, to the ruthless opportunist of the new triumvirate, to the victor of Philippi, generous in victory whilst consciously revising the history of the civil war in his own interest. But ambiguity of the sort that Rabkin and Bloom find in Caesar speaks either of a disqualifying inability to make up one's mind, or of an inertness of any impulse that can respond to the play at the level of its own radicalism.

59

To dethrone Caesar is not only to call into question the authority and reputation of the most admired figure in antiquity; it is to subvert the claims of antiquity itself to rule over later civilizations. For with that authority was handed down a theory of culture and civilization that antiquity had of itself and bequeathed to the Renaissance: the theory of cultural decay. According to this theory, art, culture and civilization are subject to a law of gradual decline. They may be renewed from time to time, but the general direction is downhill. The theory, which is perhaps derived from pantheistic religion, with its myths of gods, demi-gods, a race of supermen or titans, heroes and finally mere mortals, divided all literature into periods corresponding to precious, semi-precious and base metals: gold (Caesar, Virgil, Cicero, Horace, Ovid, etc.), silver (Tacitus, Juvenal and co.), and bronze (all later authors).

Shakespeare gives a nod to this theory, and to its co-relative theory of history's 'golden age'; but it is doubtful if he ever really subscribed to it. Perhaps it was an advantage to have only 'a little Latin, and less Greek'. He could beat Horace at his own game, boasting that his poetry would outlive whole civilizations.

Julius Caesar demolishes the theory whilst seeming to endorse it. Perhaps this is one of the play's most suggestive ambivalences. Brutus and Cassius are both dominated, it seems, by a worship of their ancestors; but actually these ancestors are like those figures in pre-Norman Britain, Alfred the Great and Edward the Confessor, whom Prynne and Hampden invoked against the tyranny of Charles I.

Perhaps it is more than symbolic that this play was first performed in the year of Cromwell's birth. It is perilous and sometimes a little pointless to search in this or that event, such as Petrarch's climbing a mountain, for the birth of modernity.

Nevertheless, one feels instantly in *Julius Caesar* the birth pangs of a new England, confident of its own resources, anxiously searching its own conscience, trying to do what is right, reaching out towards science and away from superstition. After 400 years, that England has exhausted itself, and waits for a new revolution – for which *Julius Caesar,* which has suffered a decline in popularity in recent years, might yet turn out to be a very timely play.